The
JOSSMAN
METHOD

Conquering Life's
Transitions

TRAVIS NEVILLE

THE JOSSMAN METHOD: CONQUERING LIFE'S TRANSITIONS

1405 SW 6th Avenue • Ocala, Florida 34471 • Phone 352-622-1825 • Fax 352-622-1875
Website: www.atlantic-pub.com • Email: sales@atlantic-pub.com
SAN Number: 268-1250

Although the author and publisher have made every effort to ensure that the information in this book was correct at press time, the author and publisher do not assume and hereby disclaim any liability to any party for any loss, damage, or disruption caused by errors or omissions, whether such errors or omissions result from negligence, accident, or any other cause.

Library of Congress Control Number: 2020002351

Printed in the United States

PROJECT MANAGER: Katie Cline
INTERIOR LAYOUT AND JACKET DESIGN: Nicole Sturk

TABLE OF CONTENTS

PREAMBLE

I don't intend anything written here to become some type of reference piece. I'm no expert. If you want that, go investigate Dr. Jordan Peterson; that guy is awesome. In fact, lots of what I'm writing here is heavily inspired by him. He's just so much more polished than I am. He's super intelligent, sharp-dressed, etc. I admire all of that, but that's not what this book is going to be. I wear jeans, hoodies, and lots of camo. Yes, I have a master's degree, but I really enjoy dropping F-bombs. It adds so much more color to the art I try to spew from my face. I don't fall on the other end of the spectrum either, even though I'll work directly from a lot of Jack Donovan's stuff. My intention is to simply tell you what tools I use to help my day go better and how I make myself feel happier. If I can find common ground with you by using the work of my contemporaries, I'll do it.

Bottom line is this: life is hard. You'll deal with crisis. You know what? Rather than crisis, let's use the term "transition"—that's more appropriate. A crisis is the initial event, but the hard part is dealing with it. Your real struggle will be during the transition from the old normal—which that crisis just sent to hell—to your new normal. The injury sucks, but the healing and recovery are the true challenges. You've got to learn to look at these sometimes-massive changes as opportunities to make your life better.

If you're lucky, you'll never go through a major traumatic transition in your life. I suppose that's possible, but, to steal a Peterson theme, I suggest you prepare your boat, because the flood is coming. You can't stop every problem from coming your way. Take death and taxes, for example; all you can do is make sure you're ready as fuck. I've been through the dissipation of a few serious relationships, lost jobs, been to jail, and have even had people die. It's during these transitions that I've needed the kind of help that I'm trying to offer with this book. Comments like "Keep your chin up" and "there are more fish in the sea" have always had only a momentary impact on me at best. In order to counter the depression, anxiety, and massive blows to my self-esteem that these traumatic times caused, I decided to take a structured approach to pushing through the down times.

That's what this book is—it's a look at the habits I have used to pull myself through my toughest transitions.

THE JOSSMAN METHOD

When I wake up in the morning, I don't naturally feel good. I don't have a built-in, default mode of happiness. If you're lucky, you wake up next to a beautiful woman with whom you're deeply in love. Regardless, waking up, with few exceptions, sucks by nature. Most people have an alarm clock that they may or may not pay attention to. It generally emits a somewhat abrasive tone that jolts you from a peaceful, warm sleep. Since this is such an unnatural and uncomfortable time in your day, you've got to try to leverage your self-discipline here.

I start with the most basic of things to turn it around—smiling. I just try to physically smile. It initially feels awkward, but it generally sticks. It won't want to go away once you start. That smile teleports me into a position where I have a little more perspective on my situation; it brings levity. I quickly get to, "Yeah, I gotta get up, but look what a wonderful life I've made here for myself! Awesome woman, warm bed, roof over my head, a productive employment situation, food in the fridge, a car that runs…It could sure be a lot worse!" Remembering the times when

I had no job, food, car, or a roof over my head that I could call mine is all the perspective I need. I've made it through far worse than a fucking alarm clock. As long as I get up and grind, not only will I keep these things, but I'll probably get more.

If I make myself smile first thing in the morning, I usually have a pretty good start. Perspective and appreciation are the order of the day here. Remember not to sweat the small stuff. And in the end—save the loss of a loved one or herpes—it's all small stuff. It seems unbelievably simple, but it works. Make yourself smile. It will set a tone for the day that will usually carry you throughout the rest.

"MOST FOLKS ARE AS HAPPY AS THEY MAKE UP THEIR MINDS TO BE."

—Abraham Lincoln

Even 150 years ago, happiness was as it is now—a choice. Decide to focus on the positive things in your life and you'll be a lot happier. Beyond that, learn to trust future you. Have faith in yourself that, when tough decisions need making, you'll make them. When work needs to be done, you'll do it. In other words, whatever negatives come along in your life, you'll fix them, and, if you can't impact those things, then work your ass off to not worry about them. It's a choice you make all day, and it starts as soon as you wake up.

I came up with the concept for this book on my way to a guitar lesson at my cousin Rod's house. Great guy. Weird coincidence—he happens to live on the same road that I grew up on. I was riding my motorcycle down this idyllic stretch of gravel when I devised the concept. Jossman Road is a rural dirt road. Most sections are completely overhung with large hardwood trees. Oak, lots of maple, and, near where my house was, black walnut trees adorn the sides of Jossman Road. Seeing these trees, the English teacher in me nerded out.

I still vividly remember the countless school bus trips down the various sections as a child. I can remember riding down it on my BMX bike going to visit neighbors and just going out to have fun. I got to thinking about how strong, tall, and old those trees were and how they could symbolize the people and ideas that I lean on as I go through my personal journey from birth to the great unknown. Particularly when I'm having a rough spell, I go back to the things I know. I bring my roots down into relationships, teaching, working out, building things, helping people, etc. These are the things that support me and nurse me back to emotional health when I'm down. These are the trees along my path.

It's been 40 years since I first laid eyes on Jossman Road, and the scenery has changed a bit. There are a few more houses, and the trees are all much larger, yet the route seems somehow shorter. There's so much symbolism in this shit. Even the openings between the trees where the beautiful country sun shines down on you hold value. The first time you do anything, it seems so difficult and long, but do it a few more times and it seems like old hat. Transitions are no different. They might be incredibly daunting, but you'll conquer them all. Of this I'm certain.

This book is about finding your trees. Lean on them; swing from them; pause under their shade as needed; take your time. And, when you no longer need them so much, as long as you keep moving, your road will open, and the sunshine will beam down on you.

MY TREES

I'm going to steal a concept from Dax Shepard's podcast called, "Armchair Expert." I can recommend it, for the most part, as he's got some great points. He's got a concept that he calls, "esteem-able acts." This boils down to any activity or behavior that he can universally feel good about. The only one I remember for sure is that a workout is an esteem-able act. I thought, *Shit yes! I feel great when I workout!*

I've never felt badly about myself after some high-intensity physical activity—not once. I can agree that working out is a good thing for me. It's excellent for my body, and the feel-good hormones it pumps into me make my mind and emotions feel great, too. Additionally, I love feeling a sense of accomplishment in anything I do, and a workout is a nice accomplishment for the day.

This got me thinking. Since I needed a structured, organized way to approach a transition, I sat down and made a list of acts and behaviors that I could feel good about. Rather than just make a list and try to get there, I decided to make a points system. I am a football coach, after all. If I focus on these, they will guide me down the road to the opening where the sun will shine. The 12 items on my list are each worth a point. I score myself on the day's production before I get into bed at night. That's when I recount my day's positive works and can really feel good about myself as I fall asleep. I need that quiet alone time to be as positive as possible, because that's when I'm most likely to get down on myself. To combat that, I like to be able to say, "Hell yes, you did a fine job of living life today."

HABITS

You feel weird when you don't brush your teeth, right? Naked when you're not belted in the car? That's because those things are habits. Just like brushing your teeth and buckling your seatbelt, happiness is a habit. When you decide to lose weight, you don't just decide it once. You might have to decide to lose weight 60 times a day. Every time you become aware of your hunger, cravings, potential for laziness, etc., you have to make a decision. You have to say no to the can of pop, candy bar, and chips several times per day. You've got to make the decision to get to the gym when you get up. You've got to choose to push harder when you're working out. Set goals and get to them; do whatever it takes. If you want to buy a new car, you've got to say no to lots of small spending opportunities. You've got to say yes to extra hours at work. You must do this over and over, and eventually, your fit, athletic ass will be squared up in front of a new steering wheel. What you'll notice as you make these decisions is that the longer you make these choices, the easier they get. The first reason for this is you'll start to see results that you don't want to lose. The second reason is you're building habits. The longer you practice a habit, the easier it is to perform. And happiness is just like that.

Keep that in mind as you move forward. No matter how much you'd like to think you're the person depicted in your Facebook page, that's just a show. Your behaviors (which are a result of your habits) are who you really are. All of those thoughts, experiences and pictures are ideas that help to shape what you do, but they are not your actions. What you do is who you are. It's behaviors that you can hang your hat on at the end of the day, week, or year. What can you do that will lead to your happiness?

A DIVERSE FOREST

It's incumbent upon you to figure out what your trees are. Bear in mind that I didn't say "find" your trees; I said "figure out" what they are. Most of them already exist. You've lived your life a certain way for a long time, and it's worked out for the most part, presumably. The vast majority of your habits are probably good. There are basic things in your life that work really well. Maybe it's your circle of friends that is very solid. Perhaps you have a great family. Maybe your career is awesome, or maybe you have a great relationship. You probably have a great home, neighborhood, and hobbies. Chances are, the parts of your life that are going less-than-stellar are only a minority. But those are the parts that have led you to this book—you just want to polish up a few areas.

Maybe you're facing a divorce or another loss of a loved one. Perhaps you just got downsized. Maybe you've had a disagreement with one of your friends that will be difficult to patch up. The point is that your life, like any other kind of investing, should be diversified. If you have problems in one area, you should still have several other areas that are solid and moving forward. Lean on those at that time. That's why you've built them.

CHECKPOINTS

Before you can make a daily point system, you need a weekly goal. Before you can make a weekly production goal, you need annual goals. Start with the big and work your way down to the small. I make most of my goals about tangible items—like the beer or shoes. Those make good monthly rewards. I'll work my ass off to buy a new motorcycle. That's a great annual goal. I'll put in some serious miles when I have a race coming up. I will go to a guitar lesson every week so that I can have some great new tunes to play around the fire. I know I like *things*, but I like *accomplishments* as well. These are what guide me to come up with my daily, weekly, and annual production marks.

Like I said, I score myself on a whiteboard in my bathroom in these areas every night before bed. Then, I lie down at night and fall asleep quickly. During the time between lying down and when I fall asleep, I really relish in my production for the day. It's a great feeling. I got all these things done, and each of them is a step in a prescribed goal I've set for myself. That's my daily checkpoint.

I saw a commercial once where this middle-aged guy is talking about how at some fancy resort, he was finally able to relax. I don't know what the commercial was selling, but that guy's relief at finally relaxing got me thinking. Can I relax? Am I always a touch tense about something in my life? When I tried to relax, I found myself going down a road of, "Well, this isn't done. This other thing didn't go right, this is going to be a problem…" Not cool. That was when I first started thinking about how I needed to have positive production to focus on. If I had good things done daily, I'd be less likely to let my mind wander into negative town.

I want a Friday night (this is when I still had a job) to be about more than just not having to get up the next morning. I want to truly feel good about the steps I'm taking and the life I'm building. These days, I can have a look at my whiteboard and know exactly what I've produced that week. Five great workouts, four candidates submitted, ten pages of this book down on electronic paper, etc. That puts a smile on my face and makes it so much nicer to call up some friends and drink moderately. I'm finally able to relax! Friday is my weekly checkpoint.

Every 4th of July since before I was born, my mom's side of the family would all go to Cross Village for a week or two. Most of my uncles worked for GM, and this was when the "shut-down" occurred. That was the time when all the auto plants closed down to re-tool to changeover for the following year's vehicle models, which resulted in a two-week vacation for just about everyone. Independence Day is also my grandmother's birthday. She loved Cross Village, and nothing made her happier than to have her whole family together up there on her birthday. My uncles are all long-since retired, and Gram passed on 30 years ago, but a tradition is a tradition. It's a big deal every year that we all get together up there. Now, there are 42 of us instead of just 18. The more the merrier! It's a time of celebration (yes, Bud Light gains market share that weekend) and reflection on the events of the year. There is a lot of sitting around and talking. Once the stars come out, since my family is very musical, a guitar will usually join the bottle of schnapps being passed around the fire.

I chose this to be my annual checkpoint, because it's exactly what my family did. I set goals for production every year. I want to be able to sit with my people in Cross Village and list off my accomplishments. It feels magnificent.

It's so much better to be able to reflect on a year of growth, change, and positive momentum, rather than stagnancy. I look at all I have accomplished that I hadn't done at this time last year.

While my daily and weekly goals have to do with effort, my annual goals are always outcome-based. Instead of candidates submitted, I want to have a goal of money made. I usually try to get to X amount between January 1 and July 4. Instead of volunteering or helping someone, I generally set the goal of 8 and 1 for my football team from the prior fall. Rather than eat well and workout, the goal is to stay below 215 pounds and make sure I'm preparing myself by then for The Crim, which is a 10-mile race in Flint. I generally do a four-mile road run on the 4th for my Gram. Instead of a guitar lesson, I want to have a few new songs that I couldn't play last year.

Make sense? This is when you can inventory and reap the benefits of all your work for the year. You're throwing a party for yourself, and you earned the fuck out of it. I know exactly why I'm cracking that beer, and it tastes glorious.

2012: A TRANSITION ODYSSEY

If I'm going to try to tell you how to slog through the shit, it's probably appropriate that I tell you about some of the quagmires I've found myself bogged down by. To date, my lowest point as an adult was in February 2012 when I had several of my life pieces fall like dominoes. I said goodbye to my career of 15 years, my home, my neighborhood, my marriage, a large chunk of my friends, and, in the end, a large part of my identity. It was nuts.

I was living in Indiana and teaching high school English in a town just over the border in Michigan. I coached football and track as well and was looking forward to another successful track season. I had been married for a little over three years, and we owned a beautiful, real log home on acreage. I built a big garage garage on and remodeled several rooms in the house from top to bottom—pretty awesome.

My neighbors were all farmers. They all had land, animals, crops, etc. and were a great group of people. On Friday afternoons, I'd pack a cooler, get on my quad, and head to someone's place to gather. We'd have a few beers and solve the problems of the world. One of these people was the county sheriff—great guy. We became friends right away. He mentioned that, since I was a fit, young guy, maybe I'd like to do some training with the sheriff's department. He wanted someone who could learn the hand-to-hand combat skills that his SWAT team needed. Further, weapons training and the requisite decision-making portion would be necessary. They had an odd number, and one more training partner would make everything easier. It sounded like a dream come true. I had been working out with these guys for a couple years by 2012. I had a great life! I was a high school teacher and coach, and I got to live in rural

Indiana. But everything disappeared in a little under two weeks.

My marriage had always been dysfunctional. That poor girl—she was the only child in a dumpster fire of a household. Her mother was a sometimes-medicated bipolar. Her father was a 30-pack-a-day alcoholic. Because it's what she saw, she learned that men are all untrustworthy addicts. She also learned that women will be angry at their husbands, and that there will be a semi-weekly screaming session between the drunk parent and the crazy one.

Blame is largely a waste of time in relationships. The most important (and the only productive) thing you can do is figure out where you went wrong and see if you can work to fix it. And I definitely made mistakes. I carried on an emotional affair; I was often distant; I had trouble being warm and caring. It was just a bad combination in the end. Suffice it to say, I stayed in the relationship much longer than I should have, and I came out in pretty rough shape. Since my ex-wife was a lawyer, I knew how it was going to end. I walked away from the house. I only took my possessions, which were basically limited to my clothes and what was in the garage.

Around that time, I had started smoking some pot every now and then. Two weeks after I left her, a buddy of mine came to visit. We smoked some weed, and I got caught with it. In Indiana at the time, marijuana was a schedule I drug—just the same as meth, cocaine, or heroin. I spent a night in county jail because I had a joint's worth of weed in my home. Naturally, it made the papers. Once that happens, you're not a teacher anymore, let alone a workout partner of the local sheriff's department. And, since I didn't live there anymore, my neighborhood gatherings became far less frequent. House, marriage, career, neighborhood, some friends—all gone in a matter of days.

I didn't want to leave my wife, because I was afraid that I might never have another shot to get married or have kids. I let panic and anxiety take hold of me. It was the worst emotional state I'd ever been in before or ever have been in since. Fear had a death grip on my ass. I was miserable for months—maybe years—when I was with her. I was afraid of not having a definition of self when I lost my teaching career. Who was I? Some jobs are what you do, but teaching is one of the few that are who you are. I was a married teacher who lived in Indiana and worked out with the police department, and then I wasn't. What the fuck happens now?

It took months to start to dig myself out emotionally from this. What I had left in my diverse life investment portfolio was my family and my long-time friends from home in Michigan. I had my physical health, which I've always cared for. I also had a second career doing painting and construction that I had maintained since college. I took stock of these things and chose to tell myself this:

"START AGAIN AT YOUR BEGINNINGS."

—Rudyard Kipling

The decision to move back home to Oakland County, Michigan came upon me after a discussion with an old friend named Del. At 30 years my senior, he always had great advice and cut straight to the point:

"IF YOU'VE EVER GOING TO MOVE BACK HOME, DO IT NOW, BEFORE YOU MEET SOME DAMN WOMAN."

—Del Chamberlin

I was home by April and working full time with my hands. I can remember telling a guy I worked with that I'd lose my shit if I didn't have something to keep me busy. I was right. I don't know what I'd have done without a paint-brush and hammer during that time. From April until November of 2012, I put my head back on straight. I spent as much time with my old friends as possible, worked out like a maniac, made a bunch of money, travelled, wrote, played a lot of guitar, went to therapy, and did everything I could think of that would bring a smile to my face. I took tremendous pleasure in completing a deck or painting the exterior of a house. I spent a lot of time with my mom as well as with my sister and her family. I *chose* to be euphoric. I had escaped a terrible situation. And, though my self-esteem was fucked the hell up, I focused on what I had in my life that was going well—my trees. I'd work on the rough parts as I found my strength.

I'd love to tell you that I was awesome at recovering, but I wasn't. Rebuilding during a life transition like that one sucks ass. Don't focus on getting ahead; focus only on getting by. Make the time pass with as many positive thoughts and activities as you can. Take the time, when you're feeling up to it, to ask yourself the hard questions. "Why did I end up here? What can I do differently next time? Who do I want to be?"

A transition really is an opportunity to make some positive changes in your life. There is a vacancy there that was filled with the parts of your life that recently exited. With what will you choose to fill that void?

I chose to move home and get back with the people who had always been the best of me. I chose to work with my hands to recover. I chose to train my body to be strong while I treated my emotions with care. That's what worked for me. Maybe for you, it's something different.

As a result of this time in my life, I was able to determine a very important fact: what matters most to me are the relationships in my life. If I feel good, I'll help others feel good, and vice versa. It's just that simple. From this, I derive my definition of self. I'm a man who helps people.

Several years after this time, I began to develop the pillars on which this book is built. Having a self-definition is great, but it's your actions and behaviors that determine the definition. I know that sounds obscenely obscure. But, here's what it means: you can control your actions and behaviors. That's all you can control. You cannot control how you feel. You can, with practice, control how you think and what you do about those feelings, but that's tough. You certainly can't determine how others view you, only how you view yourself. The 12 things that I *can* control that will make me feel good about my impact on my world are outlined here. These are the trees along my personal Jossman Road, and I score myself a point every day that I execute any of these 12 behaviors. The goal is seven points per day and 200 points per month.

THE 12 BEHAVIORS

1. BEAT FEAR

It's my belief that the most common decision maker in the lives of too many people is fear. I have made a concerted effort to make sure that fear never stops me from experiencing the best in life. I talked to a 50-year-old bartender the other night who is supporting two other humans by working multiple bartending jobs. She was telling me about this man she's dating who is at the tail end of a divorce. She said that she's very much in love with him but that she's afraid that he would break her heart. The divorce, his work travel schedule, and her work schedule were all interfering factors for her.

I asked her this question: "Which is more powerful for you, the love or the fear?"

Real love—that feeling when you can't do without someone—that's rare and amazing. The more you get to feel that, the better your life will be. If it ends, that's a known risk. It will hurt, you won't like it, but you know you'll survive.

I told the bartender about Cassie. There will be more on Cassie later in the book. I got to feel that falling-in-love feeling with her, and I got to sleep next to her maybe a half-dozen times. I'd wake up in the night, realize where I was, then fall back to sleep in bliss. I knew damn well that it was going to end in a train wreck with Cassie, but the risk of heartbreak was worth it to me. Love is the ultimate goal for anyone, or, at least, it should be.

I shared that story with the bartender. She said that she had never looked at her situation that way. She had this amazing love right in front of her, and she was letting fear obscure her ability to enjoy it.

To lose a chance for something amazing just because you're afraid is absolutely unconscionable.

When I was a kid, I was afraid a lot—elementary school bullies, nuclear war with Russia, getting a shot at the doctor's office, you name it. I think a lot of parents are afraid for their youngsters, and that instills a kind of hypervigilance in the kids. It's good for the most part. "Look both ways before you cross the street, don't get in the car with a stranger, don't touch the hot wire fence." You're learning to navigate a pretty scary place. For a little kid, the world has its sharp edges—that's for sure.

In middle school, I was always super tense. I remember coming home from a dance once, and my back hurt so bad that I had to go to bed. It was the tension of teenage angst sinking its teeth into my body. I'd stand there along the wall of the gym, looking out at all those girls, afraid as hell. The scenario in my head was detailed and egregious. I'd ask a girl to dance, and she'd turn to her friends and yell, "Travis Neville thinks he can dance with me!" They'd all start laughing hysterically, the music would stop, a spotlight would beam down on me, and the DJ would start taking shots. "Everybody look at Travis Neville! He thinks a girl would want to dance with him!" In the midst of all the laughter, I'd shit my pants. Cameras would pop out, and the moment would be immortalized forever. I'd go home, and my parents would tell me, "No, we can't move to another town." I'd have to deal with the fear all night, all the next morning, and walking the halls that next day would include photos of my shit pants on every locker. Even my favorite teachers would be wearing tee-shirts featuring various airbrushed and screen-printed versions of the incident. I'd be on the announcements that morning, when the principal would say, "It doesn't matter what else is going on in the world; Travis Neville tried to ask a girl to dance last night, and then he soiled his slacks. He's in room 126 right now, and you're all free to leave your classes to go stare at him." There would be a plaque in my honor built into the floor of the gym on the exact spot where it all happened. That would allow future generations to share in my shame.

I can go on and on about where my unfortunately creative imagination takes it from there. I realize now that this makes me no different than most kids. Being embarrassed in front of your peers is the ultimate disgrace. An adolescent mind cannot usually overcome such fears. As I grew, thankfully, I learned to turn that fear into something useful.

In high school, I participated in sports. I can remember that a wave of anxiety would flood over me when I was standing near my blocks, and I heard, "Runners to your marks." I soon realized that this physical feeling of dread, the heightened awareness, and the jumpiness was adrenaline! I learned to harness that fear and even welcome it. I decided to let it make me faster, stronger, and better at what I was doing. I was right. My senior year of athletics, I put up far and away the best performances I'd ever recorded for myself.

Bigger than the adrenaline thing, though, was the anger thing. Even as a little kid, there was always a voice inside of me that was angry about the fear. I was disappointed in myself for being such a damn pussy. Maybe it was my dad's voice coming through in my mind or maybe it was my own, but that's what was happening. I was mad at myself for being afraid. There was a grown man inside me who refused to allow this type of behavior to flourish. I would never feel right about the world until I could not just control but kick the shit out of my fears.

As I became an adult, I realized a few things about the world. Fear has no practical purpose anymore. We live in such a soft, over-civilized society that there are hardly any real dangers remaining. You have to seek out danger if you want that adrenaline. Fear is almost always irrational. My sister taught me this simple tool that helps when I face fear. Use your mind to extrapolate the worst-case scenario in a given situation you're worried or afraid about. How will you deal with that worst-case scenario? What will be your move? Once you have a plan for that, it's now less stressful. Naturally, the worst case doesn't happen very often, anyway, but, if it does, at least you have a plan.

What eventually won out and became much more important than that is this: fuck fear. Fuck it right in its angry asshole. If I find myself afraid of something, I will do the thing just out of spite. If I don't want to answer a phone call, because I'm afraid of what the caller is going to say to me, I answer the damn thing and deal with it. If I'm afraid to ask a woman out because she's too confident, too hot, or she's with all of her friends, I march the fuck over there and do it. I've realized that the only thing worse than pictures of your shitty pants all over the school is wondering what *might* have happened if she had said yes. That wonder, that not knowing…it's a thing that I don't want to live with. As a more confident (and realistic) man, I know that the DJ probably didn't even have a spotlight.

And, if he did, well then fuck him. Any time I face a fear in life, regardless of the outcome, that's a point.

Notes:

_____

_____

_____

_____

_____

_____

_____

_____

_____

2. DRINK MODERATELY

"WHISKEY IS LIKE A PLAYBOY MODEL EYEBALL FUCKING YOU FROM ACROSS THE BAR. WHAT YOU DON'T SEE IS THAT SHE'S GOT A CHAINSAW BEHIND HER BACK."

—*Del Chamberlin*

My folks drank beer. So did my aunts, uncles, and grandparents. They modeled whatever responsible drinking meant in the 1980s. As a kid, I often remember my parents coming in and kissing us goodnight before they drove the babysitter home. That funny smell on their breath was what I now know to be beer. From our home in Ortonville, my parents would drive the four hours to the family property in Cross Village (just south of Mackinaw City) a couple times per year. Uncle Ralph told me about a time when he and his wife (my mom's older sister) accompanied my folks on the trip. They had a case of beer when they left Ortonville, and they had to get another case by West Branch, which was about halfway.

When I was in high school, I was always playing sports and working. My friends weren't really drinkers, for the most part. I might have gotten drunk a half-dozen times and most of those involved beer bong on spring break. Three Bud Lights, and I was where I wanted to be. Man, I yearn for those days. I don't think there's a scenario now where three BLs would get me anywhere but the restroom to pee. I didn't go to college until I was 21. As I suppose is the case in most colleges, choosing to abstain from drinking wasn't an option.

I worked at the Physical Education Instructional Facility, or PEIF. The PEIF workers were all in the same lot—former high school/college athletes who loved to be around sports. Sports and drinking went hand-in-hand. We, as a group, worked as referees for the evening intramural programs. Some of us worked college and high school football games during the day as well. Our college had an indoor football field attached to the PEIF called the Dome. Since it was so far north, winter came early, and the local high school teams lined up to schedule games at our facility all week long. Some days, we'd have four consecutive high school football games to work. Those days got *long*. I can remember a fellow PEIF worker saying to me,

"WHEN THIS GAME IS OVER, TRAV, I'M SPRINTING TO DA NICKEL."

—Jeremy Pach

The Wooden Nickel was a bar right across the parking lot from the Dome, and it was a real dive. Eighty-five cent drafts and a collection of bras hanging behind the bar were a few of the highlights of this plywood-floored mecca for Harley Davidsons. First-timers got to staple a dollar bill to the ceiling with their name on it. The idea was that if you were ever down to your last dollar, you could still have a beer (and even leave a tip) at the Wooden Nickel. What a nice thing. Like a lot of rural bars, this one carried with it a sense of well-being. It was like all was well with the world if you made it to this bar. You've got a few bucks in your pocket, you're among friends, and your responsibilities and worries are temporarily suspended.

Perhaps needless to say, I did a lot of drinking in college, but who didn't?

Drinking and driving notwithstanding, my family really did model proper alcohol usage. Not once did I see my parents or another family member get angry while drinking. There were never any alcohol-fueled disagreements, arguments, or anything of that nature. There was no shit talking or anything negative at all. And never did anyone turn to the bottle when already upset. Beer, wine, and liquor were all exclusive accoutrements of good times. You go in with a good mood, and the drinking enhances that, so it is reserved for celebrations.

I tested this once in my 20s. I can recall losing my job at Blockbuster Video. I went to my close friend Joe's house afterwards. Joe is what you'd call an instigator.

Joe said, "You need a drink, buddy."

I said, "Dude, that sounds terrible."

"You'll feel better. I promise, pal," he said.

I agreed to drink, but all I got was more upset. Disappointed and disoriented became depressed and angry. That was enough for me. Never again would I drink when not feeling emotionally stable.

Side note: this goes to show that you won't do most of what your parents tell you to do. However, you *will* do everything they model for you. Never was there a discussion about alcohol with my parents. Never did we talk about athletics either. My dad was an athlete into his 40s (holy shit, so am I). My parents drank for celebratory purposes only. I've learned that this is the best move. I am doing what I saw, not what I heard.

As much fun as drinking can certainly be, it comes with a price tag. Hangovers range from almost non-existent to fucking hell on Earth. I have woken up happy to still be drunk enough that I wasn't yet hungover. I've awakened to truly not knowing where in the hell I was, walking downstairs to a table full of people I'd never seen before, throwing up in the garbage can, and passing out on the couch. Imagine how that feels six hours later. And, as I've aged, the severity of those hangovers is not what has changed. It's been the longevity of those assholes. Once I hit 40, if I overdid it on Saturday night, I might not be feeling 100 percent until Thursday. Seriously—fucking Thursday.

I learned early on how to manage the physical symptoms of a hangover. In college, I'd wash down 800 mg of ibuprofen with a quart of Gatorade before bed. Then I'd get up as soon as I could, and I'd go run two to three miles. Then I'd come home, shower, down another quart of Gatorade, and then take a nap. By 1 p.m., I was money. Feeling great. I can do that same routine at 43, and I'll still struggle for three days—at least.

But far worse than the physical symptoms of a hangover are the emotional ones. As much as alcohol loosens inhibitions, relaxes, and calms, it's also a depressant. It will fuck with you if you're prone to depression or anxiety. By my mid 30s, I realized that I'm hypersensitive to brain chemicals shifting. If I have a weekend with my buddies and I drink too much for a few nights in a row, I'm looking at no less than a week of being terrorized by awful waves of panic or depression. I feel so badly for my various female companions over the years who have dealt with this. Neither of us even knew what was happening. Now, you already know how I tend to deal with fear, and this is no exception. I get angry at myself when I'm feeling anxious. Then I go do the things. And the things are basically whatever is in front of me. Maybe that's my ex-wife, and I was afraid to tell her how I feel. You can imagine how that fucking shit ended. Maybe it's a co-worker. Don't even mention other drivers on the road.

All of that bullshit can be avoided if you don't drink. However, you also lose out on what I truly believe to be one of the last great rituals of our human race—having a beer. I want to have a beer with my dad when he's in town. I'm going to have a beer with my buddies when we are together. I want to have a beer with my woman when she gets home from work. As awful as the hangovers can be, I don't want to lose those celebratory moments in life. And, since I've determined for myself that I'm not an alcoholic, the easy solution is to drink moderately. Just have one. Hell, have two or three. You can even have five if you spread them out a little. Make sure you eat. (That's a big one!) Stay hydrated before and after. Don't start too early in the day. Stick to beer. Make your cocktail with a weaker ratio. If you overdo it, DO NOT drink the next day.

This one, of all the 12 behaviors, is perhaps the most tenebrous. Drinking moderately is going to mean something different to everyone. The idea I'm trying to get across here is that the ritual of drinking can be a boon to your life. It's overindulgence that heaps unhappiness upon you. It's for you to decide where your ideal middle ground is. It's not hard for me to not drink alcohol. It's also not hard for me to get drunk. What takes some consideration and care is drinking in moderation. If I do that, I'm having my cake and eating it, too. Point, Neville!

Notes:

_____

_____

_____

_____

_____

_____

_____

_____

_____

_____

3. PRODUCE AT WORK

Having a job is one of life's necessities for most of us. While it's a common and likeable trait to groan a little and complain about going to work, working is a good thing. You make money, get out of the house, do something outside of yourself, interact with other people, and gain appreciation for your home. That said, wouldn't it be nice to just have money? You could wake up when you want, not have a boss, play golf all day…We've all fantasized about it. Unfortunately for me, I can't get into that fantasy. I need something to keep me productive. (Plus, golf is boring.) A job does a fine job of that. When I first had the opportunity to work from home, I found that I couldn't handle it. I was very productive, but not having the routine of waking up early, working out, cleaning up then going somewhere that allows me to produce for money was tough. I just felt worthless.

Maybe you're not like me. Maybe you don't need to feel productive in order to feel good about yourself. But that wasn't all of it. I specifically needed to get out of the house. It was so much nicer to come home than to be home. Does that make sense? I really appreciated that easy chair and hugging my woman when I had been gone all day. Neither was a big deal when I knew I could have them any time. Appreciation is the finest gift a man can receive. You don't love breathing until someone has you in a rear naked choke.

More than those, I like being a part of a chain of command within a real team. I like making decisions, leading people, working together, and helping people. As a teacher, I got that all day long. Since I've been in recruiting, I don't get it as much. I don't have a leader to follow, and I've got nobody to lead. I guess it's no shock that, two years ago, I gravitated back to coaching football, where I have a big fat dose of both. I have an excellent varsity head coach to follow behind. You probably get some of both in your job as well. With any luck, you're part of a pseudo-team. Fire-fighters, police, military, and a few other select professions get to physically work together to achieve a common goal. Those guys rely on each other, fight for each other, win or lose together, and then go drink beer about it. Appreciate that. Without it, you'll switch to baths just so you can laugh your ass off every time you fart. Just out of boredom.

When I was a teacher, I took tremendous pride in being the first car in the parking lot every morning. At my last teaching gig, I lived 45 minutes away from the school. I'd drive across that state line before 6 a.m. Do the math—that meant that I was up by 5 a.m. Had I not been disciplined about packing my clothes and lunch the night before, it would have had to have been even earlier. I'd open up the school gym and the weight room and then get a workout in. Sometimes, I'd have a few student athletes join me. Most of the time, though, I was grinding solo. There were a lot of mornings I'd brave the deep snow and ice all the way there, only to get a call that school had been cancelled due to icy roads; that was some bullshit. I'd do my workout and then go home and get back in bed. Most days, I was showered, shaved, dressed, and in my classroom prepping for the day by 7 a.m., still ahead of a lot of other teachers. I did that routine for more than a decade. Why do all that stuff so early when you get out at 2:35 in the afternoon? Well, I was a coach, so I didn't get out until after practice or a game. Second, I watched my dad get up at some ungodly hour every day and head in to his teaching job. He never told me that a man needs to do either, but you do what you see.

As I mentioned earlier, getting up in the morning really sucks initially, but it can become a point of pride. Add to the annoyance an alarm clock a razor, pants, and a necktie, and your life can be balls before you even get to work. (Skip ahead to the Finish List section for more insight on mornings.) With the exception of pants, I've been able to successfully avoid all of the above pitfalls for the past three years. It's been awesome. Sometimes, if I've been lazy, I might have to suffer through a month or so when I don't have much money around. That's *if* I've been lazy. Otherwise, I get up when I get up. The alarm on my phone is for making sure I don't miss the start of a game when I'm outside working on a project in the garage. I don't even own a razor. And I can't remember the last time I shaved my face.

I realize that I'm the exception here. I operate a remote-based business that stops and starts when I deem it necessary. Hell, I got up this morning excited to write about Producing at Work, even though doing so has got nothing to do with producing at work. Irony is so badass.

I suppose this book could make me money, but it's not likely. You know, now that I mention it, production is really the over-arching theme of this book. I need to feel like I made moves that will produce my desired results every day. One workout, submitting one candidate to a client, eating well for one day, etc. is nothing in the grand scheme. None of these are life-changers. However, if you can stick together a week's, month's, or year's worth of days of producing in this manner, you've got something.

This book is no different. I've disciplined myself to write for one hour every weekday. So far, I've been putting out two pages of single-spaced, 11-point font daily. It's now November 18. I should have a good book by Christmas. That's the plan, anyway.

Your job is probably different than mine. If you're lucky, you work someplace where the goals are set for you. Hopefully, they're realistic, measurable, and achievable. If this is not the case, even just for the sake of your own sanity, I suggest you set a few of your own. Make them effort-based things you can control that will definitely get you to your larger goals.

When I was teaching, the goals that the jackasses at the State Board of Education set for us had to do with the national "No Child Left Behind" policy. This was a George W. Bush-era modification of some antiquated education policy set down in the 1970s. Like most political moves, it was just a gimmick and was unrealistic AF. I don't recall all the details, but, in the end, if every kid in your class wasn't passing or your school wasn't achieving highly on the latest standardized test, your school would get a lower-than-passing score from the government. Sounds good, right? What's more, your building had to continue to climb in scores every year. The goal was to try to get scores up everywhere, and, specifically, to get the low-achieving, poorly funded, mostly inner-city districts to pick up the pace. If low-performing districts and buildings didn't get their shit together, the state would eventually take them over. They'd bring in a state-appointed school board and superintendent and even hire new teachers. Again, sounds good.

Unfortunately, the school where I taught performed quite well the first year. It's unfortunate because that meant it would be very difficult to improve year over year after that. And, since it was tied to funding, we'd lose money if we didn't continue to improve, effectively punishing us for kicking ass. You can Google the outcome, if you want more detail. Suffice it to say, great districts started losing money when their scores topped out. The state promptly used that money to hire state-appointed staff for the crappy districts, which were all taken over by the state due to consecutive years of poor test scores. This is *Harrison Bergeron* at its finest; all the focus goes to the weak while the strong are punished.

The above is an example of shit goals.

Goals should be effort-based and entirely in *your* control. In other words, if my daily goal were to make $100,000, I'd fail every day. If it were to get *X* number of people hired, I'd likewise fail. I can't control who my clients hire. I can only control whether I gave them a candidate. Will that lead to hires? Usually. Will it make me $100,000 by July 4? I don't know—probably. I do know that I'm not making jack shit if I don't put in candidates. I know if I keep doing those small things, big things will happen on their own, as I've mentioned.

Set yourself some achievable, measurable, controllable goals for your employment situation every day, which will lead to weekly and annual accomplishments. Give yourself a point when you produce at work.

Notes:

_____

_____

_____

_____

_____

_____

_____

_____

_____

4. HELP SOMEONE

Pro Tip: If you're feeling sad, down, or depressed, do what I call the Fast Five. Pick five people in your phone that you could say something nice to. Pick anyone. Bonus if you find someone who is somewhat angry in their countenance—they need it the most. Take the time to write each of them a quick text letting them know what you appreciate about them. You could recall a fun time you had together. Hell, just send a funny meme or gif. I still have both of my parents, so they are easy targets for me when I need to send some love: "I was just thinking about it, and I realized the sacrifices you made to be my mom. Thanks so much for putting your all into it. I love you!"

I have 65 kids and eight assistant coaches on my football team. It's never tough to find a kid who has been kicking ass to tell him about it—coaches too. I'll grab a coach who's been working hard and send him a little note: "I'm very comfortable with you coaching D-line, Gary. You're doing a great job, and I really value your opinion. Thanks for working with us."

I'm a guy, so texting is amazing. I don't have to commit to a long, drawn-out phone call filled with traditional greetings. There are no worries about making sure my tone is correct; I just toss out the info and move on—quick and easy. And you'll be surprised how those positives will come back to you when you make the small effort.

If I am even remotely able to, since I'm a decent-sized guy who generally carries a firearm, I will stop and help someone stranded on the road. I have been on the side of the road more times than I'd like. Recently, I gave a ride to a guy I saw walking away from a car with its flashers on. It happened to be my girlfriend's boss. Imagine how things went at work for her the next day. It was a big win that I hadn't been planning on.

Another example is that it's no skin off my back to snow blow a few neighbors' driveways. Once the machine is running and I'm geared up, why not? I have two neighbors who are no longer physically able to do it themselves. I have a third who is a single woman who will go out and try to shovel the whole damn driveway herself. I'll give it to her; she's pretty fit and will get it done, but the man in me is not going to let that happen.

Sometimes, when I'm *really* feeling like shit in life, I go way out of my way to help somebody. Once, I painted my mom's neighbor's house for free. I just needed to put some good out there to help me feel better. I get a point for every driveway and one for every day I spent painting that house.

"WHO YOU ARE TODAY IS NOT WHO YOU HAVE TO BE TOMORROW."

—Zdravko Cvijetic

I dated another girl last winter who was a hot mess. Cassie was beautiful, fun, and cool AF. Her kids were amazing. Think Peg Bundy but about 10 years younger—also hotter. We got along really well, and she was super fun. But that's about where the upsides stopped. Let's go through this shit-show chronologically. When she was 14, her first sexual experience went like this: she snuck out of the house, went to a party, and got drunk. A 28-year-old guy who had been hitting on her all night ended up forcing himself on her. She gave up fighting him off for fear of being beaten up and just let him finish. In her own words, she "can't count the times [she] had non-consensual sex before [she] turned 18."

After high school (she barely graduated due to attendance issues), she immediately joined a travelling carnival—you can't make this shit up! Living in the back of an airstream trailer for months on end, she had more awful experiences. Too many to tell. When the season ended, she moved into a rental house with some of the other carnies on 8 Mile Road in Detroit. Google 8 Mile Road if you've lived under a rock for the past 15 years. I could write a book about the dumpster fire that ensued in that house.

When all of that imploded, she made it back home to rural Michigan and picked up a job as a bartender. Soon, she was shacked up with a local kid named Steven who hadn't graduated from high school. Of his six siblings, he was the only one not incarcerated…yet. Some time after, she had two kids (a fine young man named Ollie and a wonderful girl named Betsy) with this guy. During these times, the beatings he threw on Cassie got more severe. She's a tough girl, emotionally and physically, so she always fought back. Like every beaten partner, she figured her fighting back meant that his beating her was not a big deal. She thought that right up until he put her head through a TV. She showed me the scar. It was fairly graphic. You go into an ER and tell that story, there are going to be certain consequences. This would end up being his first domestic violence charge. By the time I met Cassie, he was in state prison for his most recent of the same charge. I guess he really put a whuppin' on the girl he dated after Cassie. He would not be getting out for a long, long time.

Within weeks of leaving Steven, she met Nate. They got married after a far-too-short amount of time. Together, they had her third child, a beautiful little girl named Emily. I think she's 3 years old. So fun. Anyway, Nate was in county jail at the time I met Cassie, thanks to several CSC-4 charges that stuck. He had, more than once (and with more than one victim), tried to fuck the underage family babysitter. From a wife's perspective, that's not just cheating. There's *so* much more there that will mess with you.

So there's Cassie. Got a picture in your mind? 31 years old, just filed for divorce on her pedophile husband, terrible past, awful trust issues, living in a singlewide trailer with no job, no prospects, and three kids to look after. She was a walking red flag.

It was the coach in me that fell in love with her. I saw who she was down deep, and she needed me. We became very close friends. We talked for hours every day. 90 percent of it was about what she had going on, but I didn't mind. She needed an outside perspective from a positive, strong (might as well just say it), father figure.

Speaking of fathers, she called once and asked if I would take Betsy to the Daddy-daughter dance, since Betsy and

I got along so well. (Remember, Dad was in prison and Stepdad was in jail.) Naturally, I said yes! Betsy and I had a blast. I've never had kids of my own, so that was maybe the only time I'd ever get to do that.

In the three months Cassie and I spent together, I can't count the times I answered the phone in the middle of the night and talked her through a crisis. There were many long talks about her past. I'd focus her on how it's made her stronger. She really took to my style of building her up. She had never had someone encourage her and build her up rather than demean her and tear her down. We focused, primarily, on the idea that your decisions create habits, and your habits are your whole life. She had made a lot of bad decisions, so she had a lot of bad habits to break. I offered her an alternative way to look at her life, and she took to it like a duck to water.

> "THE WORLD AIN'T ALL SUNSHINE AND RAINBOWS. IT'S A VERY MEAN AND NASTY PLACE, AND I DON'T CARE HOW TOUGH YOU ARE, IT WILL BEAT YOU TO YOUR KNEES AND KEEP YOU THERE PERMANENTLY IF YOU LET IT. YOU, ME, OR NOBODY IS GONNA HIT AS HARD AS LIFE. BUT IT AIN'T ABOUT HOW HARD YOU HIT. IT'S ABOUT HOW HARD YOU CAN GET HIT AND KEEP MOVING FORWARD; HOW MUCH YOU CAN TAKE AND KEEP MOVING FORWARD. THAT'S HOW WINNING IS DONE!"
>
> —*Rocky Balboa*

When we parted ways, Cassie had her own much larger home all settled for her and the kids. Now, over a year later, she has completed a degree and is working as a nurse. She's got a college-educated man who works in law enforcement. He seems, at the very least, stable, and he tells her sweet things. She has eliminated the negative things and people in her life to a great extent and is focusing on the positives. I'm excited when weeks or months go by and I don't hear from her—that means that all is well. Cassie has given me credit for her current success, but all I really did is help her to believe in herself. She figured it out, and I'm proud of her. She's still hot but far less messy.

Every long talk, every positive "atta boy" you give out is good for your soul. When someone needs help—especially *real* help—and you provide it, that's not just a point. That's *the* point.

Notes:

_____

_____

_____

_____

_____

_____

_____

_____

5. PLAY GUITAR

"OBVIOUSLY, YOU'RE NOT A GOLFER."

—The Dude

Guitar, like golf, is one of the many activities you can engage in where there is no ceiling. You will play for your whole life and never be done learning. A video game can be beaten, a career skill can be mastered, and a degree can be earned. But a musical instrument carries with it no finish line. For this reason, I'm exceptionally enthused about it. My uncles and my dad were very skilled guitar players. (I say skilled and not talented because, while creativity helps, it's reps that make you a real player. Skill reflects time on task. Being gifted is like being tall; no amount of work will make you any taller.) Growing up watching these role models of mine strumming out "Country Roads" around the campfire or playing in a band at a local watering hole really impacted me. I was in my 20s before I picked up guitar, but pick it up I did.

Truth be told, I like to sing. I figured that out when I bought the Garth Brooks Greatest Hits CD. I can remember doing my best to imitate "The Thunder Rolls" while commuting in my 1988 Dodge Daytona Shelby Z. It had a burgundy, velour interior; I can still see it when I hear that album. It was easy for me to stay on key singing. I got lucky there. That's a gift, not a skill.

I was away at school when I decided to try to teach myself to play guitar while singing. My roommate had a guitar that was collecting dust in his room, and he said it was no problem if I tried to learn to play. I bought a beginner's book of chords and started there. G was my favorite and still is. "God's chord" is what Rod calls it. That said, I'll never forget the first time I strummed Cmaj7 and sang a line from "Night Moves." That chord, though arthritic-feeling at the time, put a wide, natural smile on my face.

I grew up with Bob Seger on the radio. My Dad loved him. His music puts be back in a safe place where there are no mortgages, everyone is happy, and the world is perfect. It's like my heart can walk out in front of me and stand there by the fire, completely safe to do so. Those nights were the core of my youth. I learned everything about how to be happy—keep your loved ones as close as possible; enjoy good music and good food; laugh; remember old friends are good for the soul; don't forget to look up at the stars. Wake and practice that tomorrow.

Between Seger, James Taylor, Simon & Garfunkel, Fleetwood Mac, the Stones, and all the other influences my parents exposed me to, music is a big part of my life. They evolved into lots of other music, naturally. Who the artists you list off are is of less consequence than how they make you feel. They transport you to a place when you felt a certain way. Even the songs that take me to when I was going through my divorce bring me peace now. I remember how tough that time was, and that provides perspective to my current life and, thus, they highlight my happiness and make me appreciate my day a little more. Playing the guitar and singing along taps into that passion. It creates a tunnel right back to some of the most influential places in my life.

If music doesn't do that for you, maybe something else does. If you have a way to learn to harness that fire, you owe it to your soul to do it. That little kid inside you needs to get out and feel amazing every now and then. Find a way.

Singing in the car is fun, but performing is *way* more fun. You know how I deal with fear, so a mild fear of getting on stage only fanned the flame for me. After college, I ran into Rod at a track meet. We got to chatting, and he invited me to his place to hang out and do some music. I didn't realize it was an audition! My dad taught Rod his first guitar lessons when he was a boy. Now, his love for making music is full-blown. He could play nearly any instrument, and his basement was a recording studio. At the time we reconnected, he was still playing with his high school friends. They were probably as old as I am now, but I was only 25 at the time. All I had was some natural singing ability, and I could strum a few chords. These guys were great musicians down to the man. Them asking me to front their band blew my mind. Before I knew it, we were playing bars, county fairs—you name it. And what a rush! If you can ever find a chance to perform in front of people, I recommend you do it. It's a great way to find out a whole lot about yourself.

These days, when I sit down and play the guitar, it's like taking an emotional break. The controlled breathing of singing is meditation. It's impossible for me to sing and play guitar and think about anything else simultaneously. Choosing a song that gives me joy (and why learn anything that doesn't?) and playing it out is cathartic. I play guitar for myself. Sure, I'll play for you if you ask, but that's not the key. It's a discipline that I can never master. It's a painting that will never be completed. It's a book I'll never be done editing. There's beauty in that. Each stage of it is valuable. Your life is that way, and music is what's playing when life happens. I make it a point to sit down and play guitar as often as possible.

Notes:

_____

_____

_____

_____

_____

_____

_____

_____

_____

6. DO HOME PROJECTS

When I was little, my dad's teaching paycheck was the only income for our household of five. Money had to go a long way, so we all did a lot of work with our hands. When we needed help, it came from neighbors, friends, or family almost exclusively. We lived on a farm, and, over the years, we had sheep, chickens, a goat, geese, cats, dogs, and a few horses living in the 100-year-old barns next to the house. We grew potatoes, corn, and hay on a large scale, and every other vegetable and fruit possible on a smaller scale. My mom is amazing at making living things grow. I keep telling her that she needs to become a pot farmer—she'd be rich! We always had beautiful flower gardens on every side of the house. I can remember neighbors saying,

"IT'S LIKE SOMETHING OUT OF 'BETTER HOMES AND GARDENS.'"

—Anita Walter

Everything was old, so it took a lot of work to make our place look that good. My dad would sometimes spend the summer painting those barns. I remember the year they both worked to put new roofs on them all. He and I built a deck on the house one year. There was a morning when both of my folks decided to put down the hardwood flooring themselves. I love to sleep in, and that's a lot of banging at 7 in the morning!

More important than the stuff they did was how they would marvel upon completion. Because he was around during the summer, my old man would get a lot of projects done during the day. It didn't matter whether it was hand splitting a few cords of firewood or building a new picnic table or a dresser for their room. By afternoon, he would sit back with a beer and smile.

"LOOK AT THAT, TEE. SHEEE-IT. LIFE ON THE FARM."
—Phil Neville

Once I was a teacher, I finally got it. Working with kids has no visible finish line. But don't get me wrong, it's super rewarding. That was how the winter went for me. And then, all summer I was able to do things with my hands that had a tangible result. I could look up and see what I had done right away. I learned quickly that there is an immense satisfaction in completing a project.

The first summer of undergrad, I picked up a job as a house painter. Man, did I learn a lot. I started taking pride in being the fastest guy who would climb the tallest ladders and do the most difficult tasks. As fun as that was, nothing was finer than looking at that home and seeing how great it looked compared to how it had when we'd gotten there that morning.

A buddy and I painted an historical home in downtown Sturgis one year. The owner was a co-worker of mine who lived there with her very disagreeable husband. She often compared herself to the house, referring to both as "old lady" or "old girl." I spent that project constantly worrying what the husband was going to come out of the house and say to me because he was a nitpicker. I can't imagine how he treated his wife. This made the job stressful, but I buried myself in my tasks. I was just finishing the trim on the front on the last day, when I saw her walk out to the sidewalk, turn around, and look at the front of the house with tears in her eyes. She was shaking her head with her hand over her mouth. I thought she was going to say she was getting divorced from that asshole. Instead, I heard her say, while staring at the house, "I can't believe you made this old girl so beautiful again."

Add that on top of my already bubbling sense of accomplishment and satisfaction, and I don't know if I've ever felt better about any construction project. Ten years later, I still drive by there to relive that moment.

When a six-year relationship that I thought was going to be permanent failed last August, I knew exactly the path I'd take to bring myself back from the heartbreak. I'd buy myself a house and remodel it to my exact preferences. A couple in their 90s had owned the one I eventually chose, since it was built new in the 70s. It was still straight-up disco when I walked in. Dash of World War II thrown in there for good measure. It was built in 1975, but it smelled like it was from 1875. There was old lady perfume in the bedroom, old man Old Spice in the bathroom, and the always-majestic Bengay/beef-roast-in-the-crockpot combo everywhere else. The house was strong, well built, well cared for, and useful. It just needed updating. Even though everything was out of date, the most important parts were working exceptionally well. The roof was solid, and all the mechanicals ran like tops. The box still had space for a few new breakers, and the basement was dry. I bought it and went to work right away. The plan was simple—take the winter to rebuild the house with my hands while I was rebuilding myself with my heart and mind.

It was during this time that I discovered Dr. Jordan Peterson. His 12 Rules for Life accompanied many a day remodeling that house. I stood up straight with my shoulders back while I removed all the old kitchen appliances. I treated myself like someone I was responsible for helping while I was ripping out the bathroom and repairing squeaky floorboards. By the time I was painting, it was "Tell the Truth, or at Least Don't Lie." And, when I finally laid new carpet—which is always the final task—I was learning to be precise in my speech.

The flood is coming. Terrible things are going to come my way, just like that breakup had, and I can't stop them. When you love, you risk hurt; when you care, you might get stung. I accept that. Rather than focus outwardly, I choose to focus on myself. I choose to make my boat more seaworthy, and thus, more prepared for the flood. As I physically made the house better, I internally healed. I asked the tough questions. I figured out where I had gone wrong, and I forgave myself. That is most important.

There's a tension that comes along with forgiveness. That's because most people confuse forgiveness with letting someone off the hook. The latter is a tacit agreement of sorts that allows the offender to go on doing what he or she has done. It's like granting impunity for an offense. Real forgiveness is not that. And forgiving someone else, I've found, is exponentially less difficult than forgiving the guy in the mirror. Forgiving yourself is a progression of ideas. First, admit, "This is a mistake I made. I have reflected and have truly seen the error of my ways."

Next, "The process of dissecting the issue has taught me a great deal about myself. I've learned what motivated me to do that (and that my motivation was a good one) and how it could have been better, had I done it differently."

It can end there, but forgiveness comes when you take the last step: "I'm not going to continue to feel badly about that mistake. I can see how continuous self-judgment and shame will only lead me down a path that brings me less happiness. I'll be better as a result of this." This is how you know you're getting to the end of the demolition, and you've made it to the beginning of the rebuilding process. When you can forgive yourself for real, you're giving yourself the keys to your own front door.

Maybe you like to work with clay, you like to decorate, or you're great at styling hair. Perhaps you are good at painting. Can you weld? If you can do something with your hands that gives you satisfaction, do not undervalue how important that can be to you, particularly in a time of crisis. Anytime I complete a home project, even if it's just cleaning the place, I earn a tremendous sense of satisfaction, and you're damn right that's a point.

Notes:

_____

_____

_____

_____

_____

_____

_____

_____

_____

7. WORK OUT

I don't want you to think that I'm some crazy workout nut. I don't have a ridiculous body. I found sports late and got deeply into working out in my mid-20s. At 43, I'm 6 feet tall, 213 pounds, and I have 17 percent body fat—that's not nuts. I drink beer, and I eat cheeseburgers. I try to live life. Though what I look like is important to me, I'm clear about what I will and won't give up. That said, I do work out every day.

Are you thinking, "Things come up that make it so I can't workout" or "I've got kids" or "I've got a job"? If so, get your shit together. If your brain works that way, if you're already looking for excuses, you might have a lot more work to do than I can help you with.

This is how that internal conversation should go. Your adult mind says, "Is there a place or time when I know my time is my own and nothing will interfere with my workout? Yes, at 6 a.m.; nobody is up yet, I'm not due at work, and I can have an hour to get after it. Okay, then that's when we'll do it."

"But then I'm losing an hour of sleep!" says your internal, whiny bitch. Then your mind replies with, "What are you doing between 10 pm and 11 pm every night that's so fucking important? You're on your phone looking at Facebook or watching some stupid TV show. Get your ass to bed earlier."

Problem solved. All it took was a little self-discipline. If you can't manage your own self-control, that is definitely going to cause your life to be shitty. Sorry, bro. You're on your own.

When I was in high school, I clearly remember a few times when I was driving to work after track practice. I felt so damn good! Like I was floating. I played lots of sports, but, as a middle-distance runner, track and field workouts were exhausting. After one of those, I had an unmistakable feeling that everything was going to be okay. My worries disappeared. Eventually, I figured out that, when I had any especially difficult workout, I was more likely to feel like this. It was a runner's high! Looking back, it's the unmistakable opposite of depression and anxiety. As surely as those two assholes will make you feel a sense of doom, a tough workout carries the potential to help you feel a sense of euphoria. Harness that shit.

As a result, as an adult, I work out like I'm getting paid to. Shocker. Unless I'm injured or unbelievably sick, I'm doing something. Disclaimer here: my employment situation is not usual, and I realize this. I don't have a wife or family, and I work for myself from home. That makes it a lot easier to get the workouts in. But, even when I was teaching and coaching full-time, I still got everything done. I just did it early in the morning.

I have four separate weightlifting sessions that I perform weekly. Chest, back and shoulders, abs and bis, and legs—I do each of these once a week. Additionally, I use the Concept 2 rowing machine, take an hour of yoga, and attend a one-hour spin class, each weekly as well. If it's nice out, I'll definitely go mountain biking instead of spin or get the kayak out to supplant the rowing. If I'm going to be working physically—cutting firewood, building something, remodeling a room—I'll replace back and shoulders with that. I've found that those outdoor, natural movements are far superior to anything you can do in a gym anyway. Plus, they're more fun, being in nature, and carry with them a far greater sense of accomplishment. I don't get to look at a physical structure I built after doing a few sets of abs.

If I had to give up weights, rowing, yoga, kayaking, cycling, all of it, and just do one thing, it would be running. I try to run every day if I can. Most days it's just a 5k, but other days I'll go 8 or 10 miles. More when I'm getting ready for a race. Running gives me the best workout. I feel exhausted after I go hard, and it's completely portable. I can do it anywhere. Whenever I travel, I scout the city for a route to run down. Even in Troy, Ohio, there are things to see. Did you know that's where the Hobart Company was founded? Those guys built family homes made completely out of metal after World War II. They're worth going to see. I recommend downtown Dallas and Indianapolis as well. Cool cities to run through.

By far the best part of running is the thinking I get done. There are no phones or people to distract me, and the blood running through my body is plentiful and well-oxygenated. Add to that the feel-good hormones of a runner's high, and my mind becomes a wonderful place when I'm running.

I work out enough to stay fit enough to still be able to workout. I need to be active to feel good, so I had better make sure I can still do it. If I tip past 240, running is a lot harder. That said, there's a full-length mirror that I see when I get out of the sack. I like looking good in it. It's a self-esteem builder. Additionally, the confidence I get from walking around knowing I am fit is positive. Plus, I know I'm physically able. If I need to lift something, work hard for hours, fight someone to protect someone else, I know I can. That's a great feeling. I have found that taking care of my meat vehicle has tremendous advantages. Working out is definitely an esteem-able act and worth a point every damn day.

Notes:

_____

_____

_____

_____

_____

_____

_____

_____

_____

8. AUTOMOTIVE PROJECT

Ortonville is situated between Pontiac and Flint, just outside Detroit. Growing up male outside of Detroit, you're going to know your cars. All of those are manufacturing towns, and Detroit is The Motor City. Most of my friends' fathers worked for the big three auto manufacturers in some capacity. I learned quickly in life that vehicles were something to be proud of, taken care of, and appreciated.

The first car I remember my dad owning was a '71 metallic green Volkswagen Beetle. Not exactly a Detroit car, but it was cheap and reliable. I remember vividly the odd pattern that decorated the interior seats, which I know now to be houndstooth. My dad drove that for what seemed like forever. He always changed his own oil. Towards the end, he was always working on it—bearings, brakes, exhaust, you name it. He had to make it last and complete his fixes for as little money as possible. Again, he never told me that a man should work on his own machines, but I noticed that he always did. There were very few things that he couldn't do himself; I admire that.

When I hit my teens, cars became the be-all, end-all of my financial and social aspirations. Having a cool car was uber important. My group of friends and I did everything from massive stereo installations to nitrous oxide kits. Wheels and tires were a point of pride for any self-respecting driver. The morning before prom, we'd all get together and detail out our chariots of choice for the evening.

As an adult, I'm still a gear head. There's nothing finer than a Friday evening in the garage with good music on. Crack a coldy, hang out with some friends, and turn a wrench—it's a great excuse to get together and shoot the shit. I can't count the number of therapy sessions I've given or received over the replacement of a CV shaft or while doing a rear-differential fluid change. Having that manly distraction tends to open a guy up. It's okay to show a little softness when you're covered in grease from the elbows down.

You see that's really what any good hobby should be: an opportunity to gather with your people and talk about life. When I lived in Indiana, we'd hang out after work in a barn and tinker on antique tractors. Hell, we might just stand around and look at them with a beer. Complain a little, get some coaching, talk some shit, and just decompress. I think a lot of those guys just wanted a couple hours away from their wives. That sure as hell motivated me at the time! Women don't like to hang out in garages and barns, for the most part. Del always told me that if I ever find one who does, and I can stand to look at her, I'll probably have found my wife. He's usually right. We shall see!

Get a great hobby that includes people. Every time I do brake jobs for my buddies' wives, suspension rebuilds for other coaches, or give auto advice to someone in need, that's a point. Now that I think about it, if I'm working on someone else's car, that's an additional point for helping someone. BOOM!

Notes:

---

9. VOLUNTEER

We all have to make money somehow. As a teacher, you work *a lot*. And those are some long days. I made somewhere in the mid-50k range for salary most years, once I earned my MA. Coaching was a lot less money. Yes, we, as teachers, got paid to coach, but many do not. And what you do get paid is a pittance. So, if not for the money, why coach? It's different for everyone. I love to help young men work towards becoming effective adults in the world. I never got to have my own kids, so those that are assigned to me through the public-school system have to do. And helping them be the best they can be is a tremendous help to me in the end.

Kids in class have to be in class. Athletes are the ones who *want* to be where they are. They come out for sports for the same reason we coach them—love. Plus, I think that, like me, they appreciate the simplicity. As a coach, I don't have to deal with having a co-teacher because my class was full of special education kids. I don't have a bleeding-heart principal or department head to contend with. There are no state laws telling me how I have to run my practice. ESL kids do just fine out there, because they don't need to talk much to be an athlete. No politics, no inclusion, no least restrictive environment, nothing. It's a true Ameritocracy. If you can do it, you will be on the field.

Point worth noting here: I'm of the mind that kids need a mom and a dad. Moms nurture, and you won't find many arguments out there against them. They are responsible for things like safe spaces, bully-free Zones, and participation trophies. Those are awesome and nice to have. On top of that, kids (particularly boys) are at their best when they have the kind of mentorship that only a grown man can provide. Young men need to have an opportunity to test their mettle. They need to learn to compete. They need to know how far they can go. How much they can achieve. "I can work my ass off, and, win or lose, I'll be accepted by my tribe, because I worked my ass off and I did it for my tribe." That's safety. It's safe to fail here.

When my kids go through a highly demanding, physical testing day like "Earn Your Stripe," that helmet stripe they'll wear all year is their participation medal. They need an environment where they know that, if they don't practice selflessness, if they don't act in a disciplined manner, if they don't act like a leader would, they will be bullied by their tribe. "That's not how we do it here." You see, peer pressure is non-negotiable, particularly when they're adolescents, so you might as well create a culture that makes it work for you instead of against you.

Like most of adult life, sports are competitive at the high school level. And, like the world, there are winners and losers. It's a little scary once you graduate and there are no more scoreboards telling you how much to value yourself. I promise, my boys, that, once you get past that fear, it's the most liberating feeling in the world. You get to decide on your own upon which determining factors you'll hang your sense of self-worth. Shoot as high or as low as you want. I hope the tools I gave you will be of use along the way.

The world today wants you to believe that being a real man is antiquated, unnecessary, and even offensive. I can't tell you how angry that makes me. I'm a man, and I am proud of it. I don't get it. A woman's feminism doesn't offend me. I want my woman to be feminine, caring, warm, etc. That makes me feel safe. Conversely, she wants me to be manly, strong, able, and protective of her. It makes her feel safe. Works out pretty nicely, doesn't it? I don't need a woman who can do everything a man can do. I need one who can do everything I cannot. Vice versa for her. The sooner we stop trying to ignore the strengths of both sexes, the better off we will be.

I'd like to contrast two men whom I admire with regard to their ideas on masculinity:

"MASCULINITY, FIRST AND FOREMOST, OUGHT TO BE DEFINED IN TERMS OF RELATIONSHIPS. IT OUGHT TO BE TAUGHT IN TERMS OF THE CAPACITY TO LOVE AND TO BE LOVED. IF YOU LOOK OVER YOUR LIFE AT THE END OF IT...LIFE WOULDN'T BE MEASURED IN TERMS OF SUCCESS BASED ON WHAT YOU'VE ACQUIRED OR ACHIEVED OR WHAT YOU OWN. THE ONLY THING THAT'S REALLY GOING TO MATTER IS THE RELATIONSHIPS THAT YOU

HAD. IT'S GONNA COME DOWN TO THIS: WHAT KIND OF FATHER WERE YOU? WHAT KIND OF HUSBAND WERE YOU? WHAT KIND OF COACH OR TEAMMATE WERE YOU? WHAT KIND OF SON WERE YOU? WHAT KIND OF BROTHER WERE YOU? WHAT KIND OF FRIEND WERE YOU? SUCCESS COMES IN TERMS OF RELATIONSHIPS. AND I THINK THE SECOND CRITERION—THE ONLY OTHER CRITERION FOR MASCULINITY—IS THAT ALL OF US OUGHT TO HAVE SOME KIND OF CAUSE, SOME KIND OF PURPOSE IN OUR LIVES THAT'S BIGGER THAN OUR OWN INDIVIDUAL HOPES, DREAMS, WANTS, AND DESIRES. AT THE END OF OUR LIFE, WE OUGHT TO BE ABLE TO LOOK BACK OVER IT FROM OUR DEATHBED AND KNOW THAT SOMEHOW THE WORLD WAS A BETTER PLACE BECAUSE WE LIVED, WE LOVED, WE WERE OTHER-CENTERED, OTHER-FOCUSED."

—Joe Ehrmann

Joe Ehrmann is a retired NFL great and was a man in his 60s when he said those words. He's already been there, done that, when it comes to physicality and toughness. His masculinity as a middle-aged man is more about feeling good when you lie down at night whereas Jack Donovan's is about making sure you unleash the beast within you:

"MEN RESPOND TO AND ADMIRE THE QUALITIES THAT WOULD MAKE MEN USEFUL AND DEPENDABLE IN AN EMERGENCY. MEN HAVE ALWAYS HAD A ROLE APART, AND THEY STILL JUDGE ONE ANOTHER ACCORDING TO THE DEMANDS OF THAT ROLE AS A GUARDIAN IN A GANG

STRUGGLING FOR SURVIVAL AGAINST ENCROACHING DOOM."

—Jack Donovan

Donovan is a 40-year-old writer of books about masculinity. He's a bodybuilder, MMA trainee, tattoo enthusiast, and all-around badass. You see, that's the difference. Ehrmann has already done the things that Donovan talks about. Donovan has yet to reach the perspective that Ehrmann has gained. Neither is even remotely wrong; both are necessary. That's what I teach my boys, and football is an excellent tool to do so. Being on this team is like being in a gang. You're protecting your tribe from the encroaching doom that Davison High School brings. Make sure that, as you do that, you build the relationships with your teammates that Ehrmann talks about. If you really dig into it, it's my job to use the Ehrmann perspective to teach my boys about the Donovan world they're about to be thrust into as adults.

Why do I volunteer my time coaching football to young men? Because it reminds me what I really stand for. Every time I give a pregame speech, I remember what's most important to me. I get back to my core, and only the strongest of me comes out. I have to be at my best when I am in front of those boys. Their eyes are on me, and they are absorbing a lot of what I say, and everything I do. That makes me hyper-vigilant that what I'm giving them is my very best.

Volunteering is an opportunity for you to act. It's easy to talk about what you believe, but it's damn heroic when you put those words into action. If you ever wonder what you truly hold dear, what is most important to you, find a place somewhere close to home to volunteer your time. You'll get the point.

Notes:

_____

_____

_____

_____

_____

_____

_____

_____

_____

10. FINISH YOUR LIST

Everyone has a list of things to do every day; some of these things are very mundane. Brushing your teeth, putting on clothes, taking a shower, driving to work, and coming home every weekday are not big-ticket, sexy items. They aren't going to impress anyone like going on a vacation might. They're not exciting things to be involved in, for the most part. However, these things, when added up, become your life.

I use a calendar on a whiteboard to make a weekly schedule that includes every daily item I have to complete. It's two by three feet, and it hangs in my office. I include things like football practice, lunch with Rusty, workout of the day, take out the garbage, appointments, etc. It's worth considering that, even though a meeting with a new client might be very important, you're only going to do that once. With regard to how it impacts your life, a client meeting is comparatively tiny. Conversely, I add Prep as well as Drive into my calendar. These are things I must do every day, and I agree with Jordan Peterson's assessment:

> ## "ANYTHING THAT'S EVERY DAY IS A SIGNIFICANT PORTION OF YOUR LIFE. THAT'S YOUR LIFE. FIX THAT."
> —*Jordan Peterson*

Let's look at his logic here. If you spend 20 minutes a day getting ready, that's 100 minutes per workweek—almost seven hours per month. That's nearly an entire shift at work. If you're doing a 30-minute commute one way, that's five hours per week and 20 hours per month; that's a half workweek spent in the car. This is a significant portion of your life! That's probably more time than you spend with your parents and a lot of loved ones. It's a big chunk—why not do it well and make it good?

If you're not financially well-heeled enough to make sure you spend that commute in a Cadillac or to prep yourself at a swanky spa every day, you can still make getting ready and driving to work a better part of your life by just fine-tuning your mental intake. Your mind is like your body; if you feed it junk, it will get weak and out of shape.

Do you listen to the entertainment/aggravation industry called the news while you drive? That's probably not wise. It is going to be full of hot takes and click bait. It's not designed to actually deliver news anymore. It's designed to incite outrage. Do the research. Take that commute time and put your mind in a positive place instead. Do some breathing exercises; get yourself centered; try a podcast; get into audiobooks; practice mindfulness.

Maybe you can bring a Bluetooth speaker into the bathroom and listen to some spa-like relaxation music while you put on deodorant. Perhaps you just commit yourself to making shower time appreciation time. "While I shower, I'll make sure my thoughts are focused on listing off what I'm happy for." Make that time reflective. "I'm glad I have a warm shower to use every day. I'm able to stand up, physically move around, and be productive. I have some food waiting for me. I have a job to go to where I can find a sense of fulfillment. I have people who love me." Say what you're thankful for out loud if you have to. Smile out loud.

It's not hard to see the problems in your life; everybody has them. The trap of "as soon as this problem is fixed, then I'll let myself be happy" is a common one. I have news for you: there will be something else negative to focus on when that first issue is resolved. And while you're waiting for everything to be resolved, your life is moving past you. It's easy to say, I know. Please don't try to change it all at once. You eat an elephant one bite at a time.

Pro Tip: When I'm struggling with my attitude, I'll sometimes make a two-column Focus List. The first column is where I put things that are to be appreciated. I always list my health first and foremost; without that, you have nothing. The second column is for opportunities. These are the things that aren't going so well. Next, I'll grab a couple highlighters. I highlight the items in each column green if I can control them, and I mark in red the things that I cannot control. Then I erase the items in red.

If I can't control it, I'm not going to spend any portion of my life worrying about it. Don't get me wrong, this shit is going to slip into your mind sometimes, particularly if it's something truly tragic like a sick family member. The goal isn't deleting the thoughts from your mind (but good for you if you're able to do that). Like so many other ideas that will make you happier, you've got to make small choices over and over. The trick is to dismiss the thoughts as quickly as possible when they do pop into your mind. You're succeeding if you do that. You can't stop the flood of thoughts from coming; you can only make your mind more seaworthy.

So, it's bigger than just checking items off of a to-do list for the day. Having that calendar there reminds me that each of these items is significant. I'd venture a guess that you'll do the client meeting very well. You'll work hard and do the right stuff between clock punches. But are you doing the other daily grind activities as well?

I try to look at my day as having distinct sections. Each I've put there to improve or maintain a certain level of happiness for me. First thing, I workout. I bring my angry rap music, and I go hard. I fill my mind during that segment with things that provoke me. I tap into my personal gift of violence and go after it.

Once the workout is done, I turn the page from that section and move to appreciation mode. While I'm stretching and showering, I'm cataloging positives and fostering appreciation.

Next, it's production time. I leave angry rap and appreciative meditation behind, sharpen my mind, and focus on working. In my office, I'm analytical, and I only allow the projects I'm working on to fill my head. If I can address the problems from the past day, I will. I tend to go after the tough stuff first—get it out of the way.

After some time doing good work, I schedule in lunch or guitar. Twenty minutes of guitar in the middle of the day will do wonders *if* you can make sure you let your mindset change with the activity. That's a more mellow thought process, so I try to disallow work from seeping into that time. I take the time to pet my cats, who love to sit near me when I play. Then it's back to work for a while.

If it's football season, after another work segment I get on my motorcycle and head to the field. My motorcycle makes every commute feel special. Once I get there, it's leader time. Now, I focus on people other than myself—no thinking about angry rap, work, or meditation. This is about the boys, not me.

After a couple hours on the field, I ride home and handle personal business. I might answer text messages, personal emails, or make a call or two. I start the grill. There is meat thawing in the fridge and fresh veggies ready to be steamed. I'll throw on some Texas country music while I cook. I allow my thoughts to wander a little and see where they'll take me. Is a certain friend popping into my head? Can I reach out to them and send something positive? Maybe I'd like to go to the cabin soon. Can I start to prep for that? Do any of my vehicles need maintenance?

When I'm eating, I eliminate outside factors if possible—no TV, no phone, just food and eating it. I taste everything, enjoy everything, and feel good when I'm done. I'm just like you, I throw on a football game or a movie after dinner and use my tablet to research things that I'm interested in while I watch. Maybe I listen to a book while I do some stretches or yoga. I do my best to let the worries of the day go away during this time.

After I lay out my workout clothes for the next morning, I go check my board to relive the segments of my day. As I mentally go through each, I recall whether or not I had my mind right. Did I get fired up, become analytical, reflect, teach, eat, and relax to the best of my ability?

It's not just about doing the things. The point is to do each portion of your day as well as you can.

Notes:

_____

_____

_____

_____

_____

_____

_____

_____

_____

11. EAT WELL

I don't want this chapter to be all about what I eat from day to day. I'm no doctor; this is just what works for me. What works for you in your journey might be different. The point is not the what; it's the why. Most of what I do is in an effort to not lose what I have. My workouts, for example, are more focused on stressing my body, while cautiously avoiding injury and dodging boredom. What I put in my body has become just like that. I must do it right 95 percent of the time, or I'll get fat or not feel my best. It's just that simple.

Some ideas that have colored my habits are in order, I suppose.

Del said, "If you don't put it in you, it won't end up on you." He gets right to it, doesn't he? It's true. What you eat and drink do not just end up on your body, but also on your mind. I went to a diet coaching session at my gym once, and the lady made some great points. One of them was as follows:

"DON'T MAKE ANY CHANGES IN YOUR DIET UNLESS YOU CAN COMMIT TO IT FOR 99 YEARS."

If you make some radical change, you're not going to stick with it—it's unrealistic. You might drop a few pounds in the short-term, but, once you stop making that change, you'll gain the weight back and then some. Plus, you might fuck up your body. I know a girl whose boobs are lopsided after she did some fad diet and then went off it—weird. Anything you can't do regularly, you shouldn't attempt to do short-term either; the long-term downside is too great.

Dwayne "The Rock" Johnson said in a movie, "We don't do simple sugars here."

He was right. Simple sugars can cause everything from increased inflammation to diabetes and cancer. Not to mention, they cause a big fat gut. Do the research. I smell what you're cooking, Dwayne. I keep sugar to a minimum.

I open every day with a quart of well water. Not because it's in style, but because my house has well water. I sprinkle in some electrolytes just for flavor. I prep it the night before so it's at room temperature in the morning, which makes it easier to down the whole thing at once. Aubrey Marcus got me going on this habit. His book, *Own the Day, Own your Life,* was excellent. I usually toss in a vitamin D supplement, since I live in Michigan and it can be cloudy for days on end.

After my workout, I make a protein shake. Pick a protein powder you like. I use Syntha 6. Then, I add some frozen fruit, ice, some joint support oils, and Lactaid (because I'll fart myself out of the house with real milk. Plus, it lasts a shit-ton longer in the fridge.) By lunch, I have a tuna sandwich on whole-wheat bread. Wheat bread tastes better to me. I add tomatoes and cheese to help out the dryness of the tuna. If I snack before dinner, it's a couple hard-boiled eggs and a handful of nuts.

Growing up, as you'd imagine, we ate a lot of vegetables that were grown by my folks right there in the same dirt I played in all day. The meat in the freezer was a gift from the animals that hung out on that same piece of property. We'd trade with other local farmers, lamb and chicken for beef and pork, which made our meat choices fairly diverse. I ate fruit right from the trees out front in the fall, and we canned the rest of the year. There was very little store-bought food, except for condiments and such. What a great way to grow up! Thank you, Mom and Dad, for choosing an environment that was so conducive to our physical health. I know you weren't trying to be fashionable; it was just the cheapest option, but thankfully, it was also the best.

I've tried to mimic this model as an adult. I have a freezer filled with locally sourced, organically raised meats. No, I don't go all hipster, head down to Whole Foods or Nino Salvaggio, and shop organic. There's a farm about 40 miles from my house, and I know the guy. He's got a butcher shop in one of the barns, and I can get just about anything packaged up and ready for the freezer. I know he doesn't use anything from Monsanto. Everything is grass-fed and hormone-free, not because it's in style, but because that's how his grandfather did it. Ask around; there's probably a guy like this within 50 miles of you. It's worth the drive every few months. I grow my own tomatoes (which are the king of any garden), and I can still get veggies that my mom grew—canned stuff, too. I have a buddy who raises chickens, and I eat the eggs. When I do shop at the grocery store, I stay on the perimeter; if it's down those aisles and in a box, jar, or can, you probably don't need it.

I'm not a low-carb guy. That said, I've noticed that, if I eat a lot of them, I'll get sluggish and puffy. Dinner is generally a big slab of beef, fish, chicken, pork, or venison grilled on my Traeger Grill, along with steamed veggies. Occasionally, I'll get after mac and cheese, fajitas, venison chili, stroganoff, and all sorts of stuff. I'll eat a cheeseburger or three. I make them all myself though, so I know what's in them. Sometimes, I'll throw in a twice-baked potato from the deli counter—Kroger does a nice job on those. And then there's beer, but we already talked about that.

Physically, I feel good. I'm strong, fairly lean, and am able to perform. I have energy all day. I don't have gas, I'm not sluggish, tired, or bloated. My emotions are strong. You see, my dietary choices are more about making sure I maintain my current level rather than improving it. I have adequate support for the workouts I perform, and I enjoy what I eat. Joe Rogan uses the term, "mouth pleasure" to describe why you'd eat something that's going to make you feel bad later just to enjoy the flavor now. It's a great term. He really nailed it with that because it illustrates the temporary nature of food. It puts things in perspective when you're looking down the barrel of a bag of kettle chips.

What's all this have to do with getting through a difficult period of your life? It's pretty damn simple. Control. Ever get angry in traffic and punch your steering wheel? Ever get frustrated and kick something? Me too. That's a lack of control. When something that is important to you goes south, that sense of impotence can be so strong that it can leak out physically. The previous are examples of dealing with that loss of control in an unhealthy manner. I've learned that seeking positive, healthy options works far better in the long run. What you eat is pretty much always up to you, and how your body looks and performs is almost entirely a result of your decisions. It's a great thing to focus on and feel good about, especially when you're in a rough patch.

Like just about everything else that makes me happy, I need to look back on my day and know that I did it right. I'll feel better physically and emotionally if I eat cleanly. Want to feel better? I'll point you towards eating better.

Notes:

_____

_____

_____

_____

_____

_____

_____

_____

_____

_____

12. CALL MOM OR DAD

"IF YOU GET SCARED, YOU TUCK IN BEHIND ME, SON. NOBODY CAN HURT YOU THERE."

—Phil Neville

My dad said that to me the day I left my wife. That terrible abusive relationship had torn me down to next to nothing. I was a shell of myself. I was so raw I could hardly hold a thought in my head. Any little thing tipped me over the edge. He and my mom divorced when I was 18, so he had been there. I don't want to make any judgments or draw any parallels to their relationship, but he had, at that point, been through a divorce. He knew the shithole I was mired in and knew the mountain I'd have to climb to get out of it. It's an awful experience, and I hope you never have to learn that.

All parents want to see their children succeed. When you fail, they feel that failure as well. Before I left my wife, I remember going home to see my mom. She hugged me, grabbed my face, looked back and forth between my eyes, and gave me a look. That look told me that she was standing right there, suffering with me. She knew my pain and felt powerless to help me. She would have changed places with me to save me the pain of all I was experiencing. She said all that in a look. I recalled this once with her years later, and she confirmed my thoughts.

> "WHEN YOU'RE YOUNG, YOU THINK YOUR PARENTS ARE SUPERHEROES. WHEN YOU GET OLDER, YOU REALIZE THEY'RE JUST REGULAR PEOPLE WHO LIKE TO WEAR TIGHTS AND CAPES."
>
> —Will Smith

Parents *do* understand. They do their level best in most cases to make you as strong as you can be. Not a one of them ever believes he or she is doing wrong. They work to overcome what they see were the shortcomings of how they were raised, often neglecting to pay attention to the things they took for granted. You overcompensate in one area, so you're bound, unfortunately, to miss another. The person who grew up poor work their ass off to make sure their kid has money. Meanwhile, they're never around like their poor parents always were. And the next generation swings that pendulum back the other way—remember that once you hit adulthood. Your parents will carry what they perceive as their mistakes with them still.

Ask any therapist who has ever picked up a fucking clipboard; your relationship with your parents is enormous. Do yourself a favor and remind yourself that they are just people. They are adults who make mistakes, just like you are. No parent ever fucked up everything. They did at least a few things (probably most things) very well. And, as for their mistakes, here's where forgiveness comes in. Help them forgive themselves. Get outside of yourself and do something for them. If you have that conversation, you'll be doing them a great favor. My mom still can't let go of the only time she ever slapped me. I have told her countless times that I had that shit coming, so she needs to let it go.

Your childhood is the base for everything else you have or have done. If they were shitty parents, it probably motivated you to be great in spite of your upbringing; if they were awesome parents, good for you. Go use that advantage to do something amazing. Run a marathon. Earn a degree. Write a book. Build a house. Climb an Alaskan mountain. Accomplish some shit. Make yourself happy.

It's on you to take the hand you were dealt and turn it into something glorious. Like the football kids, there's no longer a scoreboard. You get to decide how you'll leverage your strengths and weaknesses to make a truly great life. I've turned mine into something that I'm very happy with. Do I have ups and downs, strikes and gutters? Sure do. But, overall, I'm kicking ass.

These days, when my mom grabs both sides of my face after a hug, the look is very different. She can see that I am truly happy with my life. Just as sure as your parents carry your struggles on their backs, they'll also be exalted in your triumphs. And there is no finer triumph than your daily happiness. Isn't that the whole point?

Notes:

_____

_____

_____

_____

_____

_____

_____

_____

_____

_____

SOME FINAL THOUGHTS

These 12 behaviors are the things that will lead me to the goals I've set for myself. They're tailored to *my* goals and to what makes *me* feel good. It's my hope that, by sharing the things I do and why I do them, I've helped you to start to develop some ideas for your goals and the prerequisite behaviors. Think and feel your way through this process. Be patient and realistic; don't get too grandiose, or you'll never measure up. Or, worse yet, you'll start out okay, but then fall off. Maybe you can only come up with two behaviors to start off with that you know you'll maintain. That's fine! You can add more as you grow and change.

It's worth noting that it took me over a year to dial in my list of behaviors, and I've done a lot of tweaking since that time. For example, even though it's the first one I mentioned in the book, "Beat Fear" was actually the most recent addition to my list. Just like so many things, the process reflects the real improvement. All that time working through it helped me to really pay attention to that ultimate goal of being happy. Did that behavior actually improve my day in some way? If not, toss it out. Dig in and be honest. If it doesn't help you feel good about yourself, don't do it. If that behavior does bring a sense of accomplishment, happiness, or levity, go for it.

ABOUT THE AUTHOR

Travis Neville has a bachelor's degree in education from North-ern Michigan University and a master's degree in education from Oakland University. He has had a diverse and successful career in several fields including the building trades, public education, and staffing. He is the founder of Contractor Placement, a unique com-pany devoted to finding and placing talented individuals in the field of building trades.

The author working on a brake job for a friend.

Travis currently resides in small-town Michigan, very close to the area that is this book's namesake. He enjoys the outdoors, automobiles, and coaching high school athletes. He is passionate about helping anyone in need and believes strongly that improving your situation starts with your attitude. He truly hopes that this book and the unique outlook on life's challenges it offers can help its readers.

To the Social Justice Warriors:

It's not difficult to find things to be outraged about. This book was about the opposite of that. I'm trying to show you how to find the good in whatever comes into your field of vision. If what I wrote came off as homophobic, sexist, racist, age-ist, fat-ist, lazy-ist, or in any other way hurts your feels, that was not my intent. Read that last part again—that was not my intent. On the other hand, I am somewhat entertained that what I've said got you all worked up. How, in a book about how to make yourself happy, did you manage to find only butt hurt?

Cheers.